D1235030

A Guide to Historic Bluffton

Published
By
The Bluffton Historical Preservation Society
Bluffton, South Carolina

Foreword

The last copies of the Bluffton Historical Preservation Society publication "The Longer Short History of Bluffton, South Carolina and It's Environs" were sold in 2004. Written in 1988,it was an illustrated guide and short history of the town area and old St. Luke's Parish. The need to publish a similar book has become very evident in the last two years with the great increase of tourists and residents and interest in the Town's National Register Historic District.

There is now much more information about the architecture of the structures and history of the area. Houses and commercial structures have been preserved and renovated. Sources for this book include The Bluffton Historical Preservation Society Caldwell Archive and its previous publication "The Longer Short History of Bluffton, South Carolina and It's Environs", "Historic Resources of the Low Country A Regional Survey of Beaufort County, SC, Hampton County, SC, Jasper County, SC" published by Low Country Council of Governments, 1990 and the National Register of Historic Places United States Department of the Interior, National Park Certification of Bluffton Historic District,1996. Many individuals with information about families and properties have also contributed to this book.

Several members of the BHPS have undertaken the task of compiling information, adding and updating text, photographs and maps to add to the basics of the excellent earlier book. This book, "The Guide to Historic Bluffton" has been compiled and edited by Ann Elliott, Donna Huffman, Mary Reeves and Lucy Scardino. Cecelia Caldwell has provided editing assistance. An invaluable addition to the text of this book is the work of Ben and Betsy Caldwell, Hunter Saussy and others who assisted with the 1988 publication.

Donna Huffman is responsible for the design and layout of this book.

 They vary in the date taken – some are very old and others current. Many were taken by Ben Caldwell for the "Longer Short History of Bluffton and It's Environs." Current photographs include pictures taken by Ed Funk and Donna Huffman.

Drawings by Naomi McCracken and Christina Bates are used with special permission.

Tour maps throughout the book were prepared by Donna Huffman and Lucy Scardino. Arthur Elliott, III gave permission for use of his hand drawn map of St. Luke's Parish with modern county, town and road overlays.
The information in this book is true and complete to the best of our knowledge.

Map on the inside front cover and chapter sections from the South Carolina Land Improvement Co. 1877.
Cover Image: The Cole-Heyward House, Ed Funk photographer

ALL HOUSES ARE PRIVATE RESIDENCES EXCEPT THE HEYWARD HOUSE HISTORIC CENTER AND ARE TO BE VIEWED FROM OFF THE PROPERTY ONLY.

Contents

The Bluffton Historical Preservation Society 6

A Short History of the Bluffton, South Carolina Area............... 8

The Bluffton Movement.. 12

Civil War Action in Bluffton... 14

South Tour 19

North Tour 33

East Tour 43

West Tour 55

Outlying Area Historic Structures 69

Books of Interest 79

Fold Out Map.. Back Cover

The BLUFFTON HISTORICAL PRESERVATION SOCIETY, Inc.

"The Bluffton Historical Preservation Society, Inc. was organized in 1981 at Bluffton, South Carolina by W. Hunter Saussy and sixteen other interested residents of the town. From that modest beginning our membership has grown to hundreds of interested people. Many of these are descendents of early families of the area.

The Society's constitution states its purpose: 'To bring together people interested in history, and especially in the history of Bluffton and its vicinity'. Our major function is to discover and collect any material which may help to establish or illustrate the history of this area. The Society will provide for the preservation of such material and make it accessible as far as may be possible, to seriously interested persons who wish to examine or study it. The Society also will undertake the preservation and marking of historical buildings, sites and monuments. The Society seeks to arouse interest in the past by furnishing historical information to newspapers and other media and by holding meetings with lectures and papers presented and discussed.

Members and friends of the Society have been collecting, researching, writing and editing material for a definitive history of old St. Luke's Parish and its residents from the 1700s to the outbreak of the War Between the States. Searching through dusty files and crumbling public records, pursuing leads, inventorying cemeteries, interviewing folks, photographing buildings, sites, cemeteries and old photographs, deeds, wills, etc. ...wherever history can be found and documented we are there digging. We hope that one day we will publish what has become known as "The Big Book" and to have a place where the burgeoning collection of files, photographs, maps, drawings, relics, memorabilia, and other historical data can be displayed and studied."

Excerpted from The Longer Short History of Bluffton, South Carolina and its Environs, originally published by the Society in 1984.

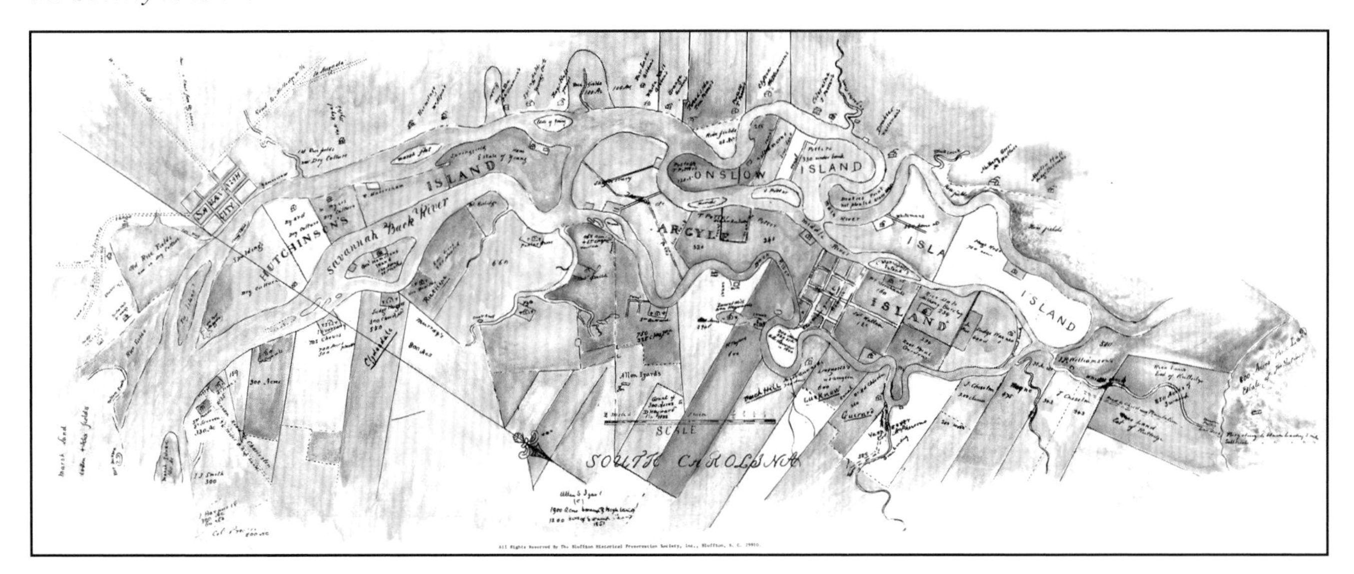

1851 Map of South Carolina Savannah Back River Plantations

The Society continues its focus on historical research, collecting items to add to the archives and providing historical information to the community. In 1986 we placed 10 historical markers on the antebellum structures in Bluffton. These were replaced in 1999 and 17 additional markers placed on other buildings of historic interest. Tours sponsored by the Society opened the interiors of historic and other homes to expand the interest and knowledge of the area as well as providing additional funds for the Society's projects.

The Society continued focusing on historical research, collecting items to add to the archives and providing historical information to the community. In honor of Ben and Betsy Caldwell, The Society created the **Caldwell Award** in 1997 to recognize persons who have made outstanding contributions to increase the awareness of the importance of history and the preservation of historic places in Bluffton. The first award was presented to Betsy Caldwell for her tireless interest in increasing the knowledge of family and area history and her leadership in developing this Society into the outstanding organization it has become. In 1999, the award was given to Mr. and Mrs. Van DuBose for the preservation of the Seabrook House. Roberts Vaux received the award in 2000 for the preservation and adaptive reuse of the commercial Deer Tongue Building. Mr. and Mrs. Robbie Cahill renovated the Orage Cottage and received the award in 2002. The award was presented to Mr. & Mrs. Peter Lamb (Lucy Scardino) in 2005 for their restoration of the Prichard House.

The opportunity to fulfill the Society's purpose to undertake the preservation of historical buildings occurred in 1998. Several historic homes in Bluffton had recently been sold and the Society became increasingly aware of the need to become involved in the preservation of such structures. In February 1998, the decision was made to purchase the Cole-Heyward house at 70 Boundary Street from Mrs. Hasell Heyward. This fine example of a Carolina farmhouse was built circa 1840 by John J. Cole, the owner of Moreland Plantation on the May River Neck (*now known as Palmetto Bluff*). A limited partnership was formed to purchase the property and to lease it to the BHPS, for the Society to operate as the Heyward House Historic Center. In 2000, when the mortgage was assumed by the BHPS, plans to make it a house museum became a reality and historic restoration began. Tours of the house and slave quarters began almost immediately.

The house was designated as an official project of the ***"Save America's Treasures"*** and in 2002, it also became the official welcome center for the Town of Bluffton. The preservation of this house, has raised the awareness of the need for preservation of the entire town (which was added to the National Register of Historic Places in 1996).

The Cole-Heyward House provides a rare glimpse into antebellum construction as a continuing preservation project and educational opportunities in antebellum life to thousands of visitors yearly, including local school children and adults from around the world.

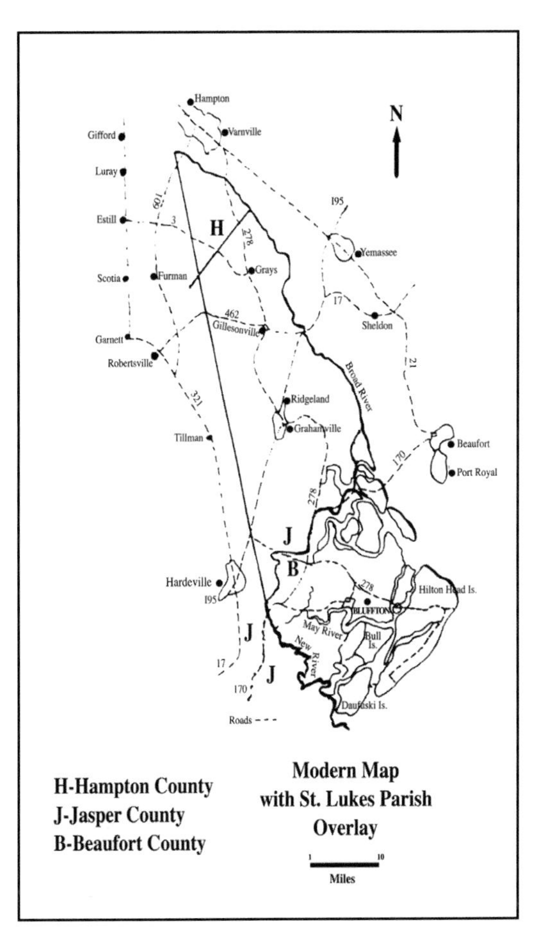

Modern Map with St. Lukes Parish Overlay

A SHORT HISTORY OF THE BLUFFTON, S.C. AREA

To understand the history of Bluffton it is necessary to have some knowledge of its geographic location and the history of adjacent areas such as Hilton Head, St. Helena, Port Royal and other barrier islands for the people who first settled Bluffton were of the same families that earlier developed those places.

While Port Royal, St. Helena and Hilton Head were first explored by the Spanish in 1520, the French in 1562 and finally colonized by the English in 1670, the lower part of what is now Beaufort County, which includes the Bluffton area, were considered "Indian Lands". This situation existed until after the Yemassee Indian War which began in 1715. After a long, sporadic and bloody struggle the Yemassees and their Indian allies were finally defeated in 1728 and removed from the area; with the majority of the surviving Yemassees going to what is now south Georgia and Florida where they were absorbed into the Seminole tribe.

After the removal of the Yemassees the area was opened for settlement by white colonists. Purrysburg, on the South Carolina side of the Savannah River, was settled by Swiss colonists in 1732 and Savannah was settled in 1733 by the English under General Oglethorpe.

Before these settlements were formed, the Lord Proprietors who controlled the Carolinas under a charter from King Charles II, granted themselves in 1718 additional baronies of approximately 13,000 acres each in these formerly "Indian Lands". The Devil's Elbow Barony, which covered an area between the Colleton and Okatie Rivers on the north, the May River on the south, Mackey's Creek on the east, and a line drawn from Linden Plantation on the May River to and including Rose Hill plantation on the Oketee [sic] River, was drawn by lot by Sir John Colleton and deeded to him on December 5, 1718.

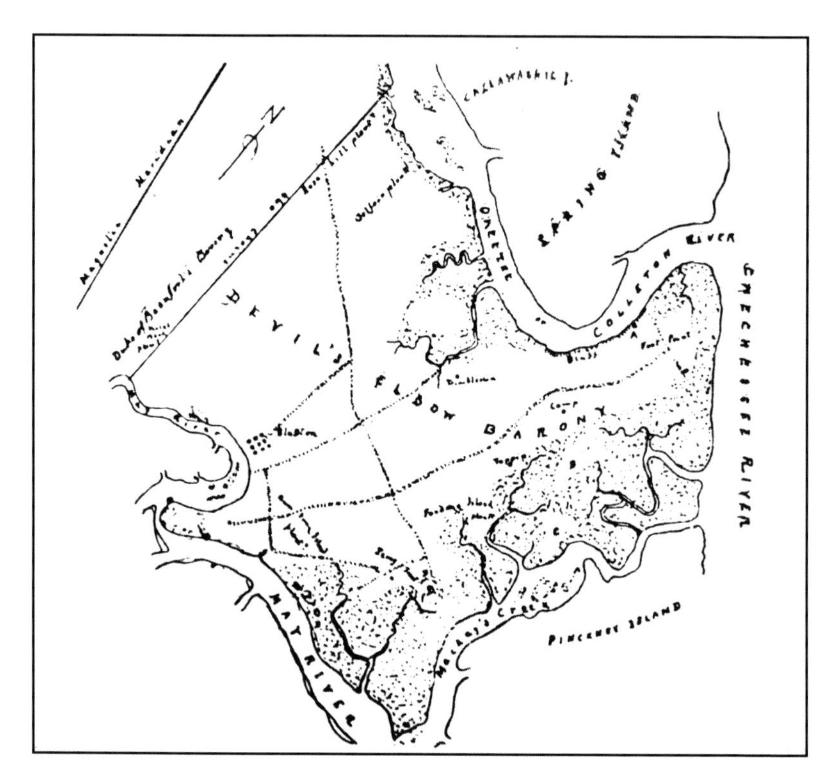

Devil's Elbow Barony

The original Sir John did very little with this barony as he had other and more developed baronies in other parts of the Carolinas including his main barony, Fairlawn in what became Berkeley County near Charleston. Finally his grandson, also a Sir John Colleton, did develop some plantations in the Victoria Bluff – Foot Point areas. These plantations were destroyed by the British under General Provost in 1779 during the American Revolution.

This Sir John Colleton died in 1776, but prior to his death he divided the western half of Devil's Elbow Barony into six tracts and sold them. A tract of 680 acres, which included the present town of Bluffton went to Benjamin Walls.

Following the Revolutionary War, and with the invention of the cotton gin at Mulberry Grove plantation on the Savannah River, cotton and particularly long-staple cotton grown on the sea islands, became the chief money crop of the island plantations; and, together with rice grown on the mainland plantations bordering the fresh water rivers; the Savannah and New Rivers, brought great prosperity.

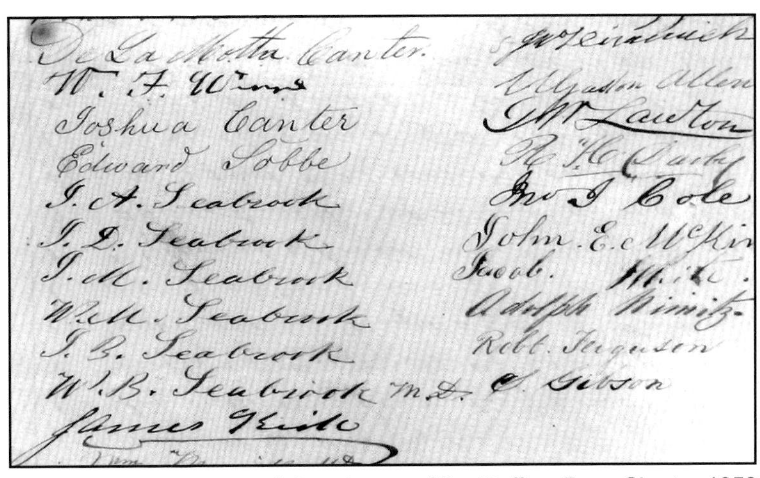
Joshua Canter
I. A. Seabrook
I. D. Seabrook
I. M. Seabrook
Wm. Seabrook
I. B. Seabrook
Wm. B. Seabrook M.D.
Jno I. Cole
Robt. Ferguson

A few signers of the Bluffton Town Charter 1853

Summers on a plantation and especially on a rice plantation were not the most healthful. The intense heat and hoards of malaria and yellow fever carrying mosquitoes brought illness and death, primarily to the white population of the plantations. It was for this reason that wealthy planters began to look for a healthier place to keep their families. And the area we now call the town of Bluffton was the ideal choice. With its high bluff and huge spreading live oak trees and facing directly into the prevailing cool, southeast summer breezes, the area had the healthful climate they sought. It was also easily accessible by water to their working plantations on the islands and on the mainland.

So began the real history of Bluffton. The first summer homes were built here in the early 1800s. There is evidence of the Pope and the Kirk families being here shortly after 1800. Unfortunately information on the period between the American Revolution and up to 1860 is very scanty. All of the Beaufort County Court House records of the period were destroyed by General William Tecumseh Sherman's cavalry in 1865 while being moved from the Court House in Gillisonville to Columbia for safekeeping. Our main source of information of the antebellum period comes from old family letters, a few memoirs written by persons who visited the area, some church records, wills and some articles in the Savannah and Charleston newspapers of that time.

We do know that the healthy climate and beauty of the area began to draw more and more planters here, not only for summer (April-October) but for year-round residency. Sometime during the 1830s the town was formally laid out under a street plan that still exists today.

In the period between the 1830s and 1860s Bluffton continued to grow. It was first known as "May River", then later as "Kirk's Bluff". In the early 1840s a mass meeting was called under the leadership of R. Barnwell Rhett to have the village change its name to Bluffton for the high banks on which it stands and as a compromise between the Kirk and Pope families, each of which wanted the town named for them. The first reference to "Bluffton" appeared in an advertisement in the Savannah paper of July 1843: 'of boat service to Bluffton'.

Two large churches, one Episcopal and one Methodist, were built and a private school was started by Prof. Hugh F. Train, a Scotsman brought over to tutor the children of the wealthy planters. The poet Henry Timrod also taught in this private school. Several stores started on Calhoun (then Main) Street and a Masonic Lodge was organized.

Bluffton as a town was finally chartered in 1853.All of this affluence came to a grinding halt with the outbreak of the War Between the States and the capture of Hilton Head Island by Federal forces on November 17, 1861. Most of the white population fled temporarily to Bluffton but due to the Federal Navy's control of the sounds and rivers and the ever present fear of raids by Federal troops and gun boats, the entire population of Bluffton was soon evacuated to safer havens in the interior such as Grahamville, Gillisonville, Allendale, etc. Bluffton became a deserted place with homes, furniture and belongings all abandoned.

During 1862 Federal troops and gun boats visited Bluffton on three occasions, but other than removing furnishings from the deserted houses which they used to furnish their quarters at Fort Pulaski the town was not damaged.

During this period the town was used by Confederate forces as a headquarters from which pickets, or lookouts, were distributed at various points along Calibogue Sound and the May River. These pickets were to report any movements by the Federals up the May River to the Confederate cavalry stationed at Pritchardville, about eight miles west of Bluffton.

Early in June of 1863 General David Hunter, the commander at Hilton Head, ordered Colonel Barton, the commander at Fort Pulaski to take his troops and destroy the town of Bluffton. Without going into detail as to the military operation involved, as this is another full story in itself, the town was set on fire and apparently two-thirds of the houses, including most of the better ones along the bluff were destroyed on June 4, 1863. The two churches and approximately fifteen of the residences in the center of the town escaped destruction. Of these, two churches and eight houses remain today.

After the war, with their houses burned, their Hilton Head plantations confiscated by the Federal government, and their rice plantations along the New and Savannah Rivers in ruin, many were bankrupt by the war and their Bluffton properties were sold for taxes.

Some families did return, however, and these together with new people who moved in from other parts of the state, primarily from Hampton, Colleton and Beaufort counties and a few from the North, began to rebuild Bluffton. This time the people were mainly merchants, not planters, and in time Bluffton became the commercial center for this part of Beaufort County; with an economy tied very closely to the May River and forest products. Bluffton also continued to draw many summer visitors to their homes along the bluff. By the early 1900s Bluffton boasted seven or eight large general stores along Calhoun Street carrying everything the people needed to sustain themselves, from hardware and dry goods to molasses and groceries. Practically everything that came into and left Bluffton did so by river boats which maintained regular passenger and freight services between Savannah and Bluffton with stops at Daufuskie Island, Spanish Wells, and Palmetto Bluff then known as "Halsey's". Bluffton was once again a prosperous, peaceful and healthy place in which to live or vacation.

This second phase of Bluffton's history came to a close following the building of the Coastal Highway, (US17), and the bridging of the Savannah River at Port Wentworth in 1926. People living in the area could now drive to Savannah for their shopping; freight now arrived and left by trucks; and the river boats which were such a vital and picturesque part of Bluffton's past disappeared from the scene. Bluffton as a trading center began to decline.

Bluffton, as in the past, continued to draw summer residents who treasured the cool breezes and general beauty of the May River estuary. However it was the development of Hilton Head Island and the bridging of Mackey and Skull Creeks in the 1950s and the building of the Talmadge Bridge and the short route to Savannah which brought prosperity back to the area.

Today people say, "Bluffton is a way of life" or, "Bluffton is a state of mind". In either case, Bluffton with its historic past, its beautiful bluff and river estuary, its healthy climate, and its quiet peaceful atmosphere, continues to charm everyone who will take the opportunity to visit it.*

**Based on a talk given by W. Hunter Saussy, Founder and President Emeritus, at the first general membership meeting of the Bluffton Historical Preservation Society, 31 January 1982.*

It might be said that Bluffton's third phase began with the area's rapid development in the 1990s. Beginning with the opening of Sun City Hilton Head at Hwy. 170 and 278, then came development of large gated communities, accelerating along the north side of 278. Bluffton citizens desiring to control and benefit from additional development that was destined to come, annexed approximately 53 square miles of land to the north, west and south of the original one-square mile town. The 20,000+ acre Palmetto Bluff tract across the river and the Shults tract immediately north of the town center were the first to be voted into the town. While planning was undertaken and infrastructure was being installed on these two tracts, the Buckwalter and then the Jones tracts were annexed. All of these lands are being developed for residential, commercial and and civic uses. Population increases in the town proper and surrounding Bluffton Township means an increase in the importance of Bluffton in the economic, cultural and educational life in southern Beaufort County. Simultaneously, preservation of the National Register for Historic Places district at the core of the old town and environmental conservation of the May River are being addressed so that the beautiful bluff, pristine May River and restored and adaptively reused old town structures will continue to charm all who live and visit here.

The day excursion boats The Louise and The Attaquin at the Town dock, c.1920.

THE BLUFFTON MOVEMENT

by Janice Hunter Cantrell*

One of Bluffton, South Carolina's great claims to historical fame is that under one of its great oaks on July 31, 1844 "The Bluffton Movement" for secession was born and led to South Carolina's withdrawal from the Union on December 20, 1860 – the first state to secede.

The great issues of the times that were so onerous to the South and so vigorously promoted by the Union were: the slavery question, state's rights, the 1828 and 1842 Federal tariffs which so oppressed southern planters, and the proposed annexation of Texas and the acquisition of Oregon and California.

All of these were highly controversial. They were sectional issues. And what was good for the North was usually thought not to be good for the South, and vise versa. Fortunately, however, at least for several years, there were some on both sides who sought to solve the great questions amicably and fairly. Years were earnestly spent by southern politicians and statesmen to find ways to allow the perpetuation of slavery on which the entire economy of the South was based; to reduce the tariffs to revenue measures only; and to recognize the constitutionality of the rights of the individual states.

The Secession Oak

Simultaneously with these efforts, attempts were made to create a Confederation of Southern States which some thought would be better able to deal with the North than could individual states. Even temporary secession was considered, the idea being that this might bring the North to the conference table. But there was no unified effort, so for years the South's problems remained unsolved.

Finally, in desperation, prominent men of Bluffton and St. Luke's Parish formed a committee to call a meeting at which Robert Barnwell Rhett, congressman for the district, and others would speak to the problems which had long plagued the South.

The committee consisted of: the Honorable William Pope, President; the Honorable Benjamin Franklin Scott; Dr. George Mosse Stoney and William H. Wigg, Esq. Vice Presidents; George Allen, George P. Elliott and William H. Wigg were in charge of invitations. Other members were Dr. James William Kirk, Thomas Drayton and Capt. Burrell Wiggins.

When July 31, 1844, the appointed day arrived, a crowd, (estimated in some accounts at 500), assembled under the now famous oak in Bluffton to hear Robert Barnwell Rhett, who had been so vociferously agitating since the 1820s for 'Nullification (of the tariffs), or Secession', that he was known in the North as "the enfant terrible". There was much speechmaking and toasting and spirits were high.
Various accounts differ as to how lasting was the effect of "The Bluffton Movement", depending on who was the author and what his feelings were toward Rhett who was regarded by some as an extremist and a South Carolina hotspur, but was eventually termed 'father of secession' and had a strong following.

History tends to show that "The Bluffton Movement" did not subside but was a strong catalyst among the forces which brought about the secession of South Carolina on December 20, 1860 and shortly thereafter led to the secession in turn of Mississippi, Alabama, Florida, Georgia, Louisiana and Texas, later to followed by Virginia, Tennessee and North Carolina.

**This is a condensation of the article by Mrs. John D. Cantrell, a former Bluffton resident, written for the Society's as yet unpublished book, A History of St. Luke's Parish, Beaufort District, South Carolina from the 1700s to 1860. She also gave a talk on the Bluffton Movement to the Society at a general membership meeting 21 October 1984.*

View from Huger House

ACTIONS ON THE MAY RIVER AND THE FIRING OF BLUFFTON BY UNION FORCES

Part I: *O.R.-SERIES I—VOLUME XIV [S#20]
SEPTEMBER 30-OCTOBR 3, 1862—*Reconnaissances on May and Savannah Rivers, Ga.*
No. 2—*Report of Col. William B. Barton, Forth-eighth New York Infantry*

HEADQUARTERS U. S. FORCES,
On the Savannah River, Fort Pulaski, Ga. October 4, 1862

LIEUTENANT-COLONEL: I have the honor to report, for the information of the general commanding, that in accordance with the permission granted in his communication of September 26 I left this post a 1 o'clock on the morning of the 30th ultimo, with armed steamers Planter and Starlight, having on board five companies Forty-eighth New York State Volunteers, under the command of Capt. D. W. Strickland, and a detachment of Company, Third Rhode Island Artillery, in charge of Capt. John H. Gould. We arrived at the mouth of the May—commonly called Bluffton—River, about three-quarters of an hour before daybreak, and proceeded as rapidly as possible up the river. My original design was to land the infantry force at a point 11⁄2 miles this side of Bluffton, and by making a rapid march gain a point in the rear of the village to which all the roads leading from it converge, and thus cutting off a squadron of cavalry I knew to be stationed there. Unfortunately, however, when within half a mile of this point, in the thick fog which prevailed the Planter ran aground, and the noise of the engines in getting her off revealed us to the enemy's pickets, and rendered anything like a surprise impossible. I however landed the troops as soon after the steamer got afloat as possible, and directing Captain Strickland to skirmish and scout the country thoroughly and to keep up constant communication with me through his signal officer, proceeded with the steamers directly up to Bluffton, keeping some half a mile ahead of the troops on shore. This village is one of the most defensible possible against an attack by water, as the river makes a sharp turn a short distance from it and the bluffs entirely command the narrow channel through which vessels necessarily approach bows on. We found the town entirely deserted, however, although there was every evidence that a portion of the inhabitants and the enemy's cavalry had just left. I remained here only long enough for the infantry to come up, but pushed on up the river to Crowell's plantation and Gadsden's Bluff, where I had learned there were extensive salt-works. Immediately after leaving the wharf we discovered some 200 cavalry and a body of infantry rapidly retreating down the Hardeeville road, which was skirted on the opposite side by impassable woods, but entirely open on the side toward us. We opened fire upon them from all our guns, and I am convinced most effectively; our shell exploded very frequently directly among them, and there was soon a perfect stampede. I feel certain that their loss in killed and wounded must have been very considerable. We continued firing until they were entirely out of sight and range, by which time we had reached Crowell's plantation, which had been left by its owner half and hour before.

The salt-works here we completely demolished, tearing down the furnaces and vats and destroying the kettles. Some contrabands made their appearance, who pointed out the location of other salt-works just above, which we also destroyed. These last were very extensive, the vats extending for more than a quarter of a mile. The yield of salt must have been very great. Meanwhile the enemy again made his appearance on a high bluff a mile distant with a piece of artillery drawn by four horses, but upon the first discharge of our guns they beat a most precipitate retreat. As we had fully accomplished the object of our expedition, and nothing more remained to be done, we returned to Fort Pulaski.

On our way down we stopped again at Bluffton, and carried off a considerable quantity of furniture from the deserted houses, which is now at this post, subject to the disposal of the general commanding.

In behalf of my officers and myself I would respectfully request that we be permitted to retain these articles for our use while at this post. The reconnaissance made of the roads to and beyond Bluffton was most complete and perfect, and I trust at some future time may prove useful in future operations toward Savannah. All the roads bore evidence of the confused retreat of the enemy. I learned among other things that the force at Hardeeville does not consist of over three regiments, and that there are two not very formidable batteries between Bluffton and that place, both on the main road.

It affords me pleasure to add that the officers and men of my command conducted themselves during the day in the most commendable manner, embarking ad disembarking in perfect order and with great promptness They were only disappointed that they did not et a nearer view of the enemy.

I would mention as especially deserving of commendation Captain Strickland, who commanded the land forces, and Captain Coan, in charge of skirmishers, both of Forty-eighth New York State Volunteers; also Captain Gould and Lieutenant Fry, Third Rhode Island Artillery, for their excellent gunnery. Adjt. A. W. Goodell, of my regiment, also rendered me efficient aid. I have the honor to be, colonel, very respectfully, your obedient servant,

WM. B. BARTON
Colonel Forty-eighth New York Volunteers, Comdg. Post.
Lieutenant-Colonel PRENTICE,
Assistant Adjutant-General, Chief of Staff.

Part II: (Excerpt of Report by Officer in Charge of Attack)
U.S.S. COMMODORE MCDONALD
Port Royal, S.C. June 4, 1863

SIR: I have the honor to report that in obedience to your order I proceeded to Fort Pulaski and reported to Colonel Barton, the commander of the fort, as officer in command of naval forces for the attack on Bluffton. He immediately gave orders that the army gunboat Mayflower should be placed under my command. After arranging the plan of attack, I left Fort Pulaski in time to cross Calibogue Sound at high water, and came to anchor off the south end of Hilton Head Island and awaited the arrival of the army gunboat and transports, which were of lighter draft, and were to join me at 11:30 p.m. Unfortunately the Mayflower grounded on the flats. The steamer Island City and transport Cossack, having on board about 1,000 volunteers (this ship leading them), got underway for the point of attack. On account of being detained by the Mayflower it was long after daylight before we reached the point where the troops were to disembark which was about 3 miles this side of Bluffton. Meeting with no opposition at that point the troops were landed in safety, and both them and ourselves advanced to the attack.

The Mayflower having joined us in the meantime, I anchored from half to three quarters of a mile from the town, bringing our batteries to bear upon it. The land forces having without opposition occupied the town, I moved up with this vessel and the transports for the purpose of being better able to reembark the troops in case of necessity, as the enemy had mustered quite a large force in the rear of the town of infantry and cavalry. Soon after we had anchored abreast of the town, and but a few yards from it, sharp firing was heard in the rear between the rebels and our forces. The commanding officer of the land forces made signal that he wished us to shell the woods in their rear, as the rebels were mustering in quite a strong force; I immediately opened with my guns, firing both shell and shrapnel, with five second fuze, which compelled the enemy to fall back. In the meantime the town was fired in several places by order of the commander of the land forces, the church being the only building spared. As we had succeeded in carrying out the object of our expedition by destroying the town and breaking up this nest of marauder, the troops were ordered to reembark.

Very respectfully, your obedient servant, George Bacon,
Lieutenant Commander, U.S. Navy.
Rear Admiral S.F. DuPont
Comdg. South Atlantic Blockading Squadron, U.S. Navy.

Part III: (Excerpt of Correspondence to Brig. Gen. Q. A. Gillmore, Hdqrs. Dept, South Carolina, Georgia, and Florida, Charleston, S. C., July 4, 1863 from G. T. Beauregard, *General Commanding)*

...A day or two later, another expedition burned about two-thirds of the village of Bluffton, a summer resort of the planters of the sea-coast of South Carolina, an undefended and indefensible place. The best houses were selected for destruction, and for the act no possible provocation may be truthfully alleged... In, conclusion, it is my duty to inquire whether the acts which resulted in the burning of the defenseless villages of Darien and Bluffton...are regarded by you as legitimate measures of war, which you will feel authorized to resort to hereafter.

BURNED
1. Dr. Paul Prichard
2. Colonel J.J. Stoney
3. Dr. John W. Kirk
4. Squire William Pope
5. H. F. Train
6. General T.F. Drayton
7. George Allen
8. M. J. Kirk
9. William Pope
10. B. Wiggins
11. J.G. Bullchen's Store
12. James Chalmers
13. D. & J. Canter
14. Mrs. Pinckney
15. Fred Langbaile
16. Martin
17. J.C. Bullchen
18. H. Guerard Estate
19. Joseph Baynard
20. Dr. F.P. Pope
21. Richardson Pope
22. Dr. Alexander Verdier
23. William Pope
24. J.J. Pope
25. F. H. Verdier
26. G.W. Laughton
27. Norton Estate

NOT BURNED BUT DEMOLISHED LATER
9. G. Gaston Allen
10. Rev. Joseph B. Seabrook
11. Masonic Lodge
12. T.J.S. Farr
13. Paul Seabrook
14. Mrs. H.R. Hardee
15. Joseph M. Farr
16. Mrs. James Kirk
17. T.H. Coe
19. Joseph D. Seabrook
21. William Micker

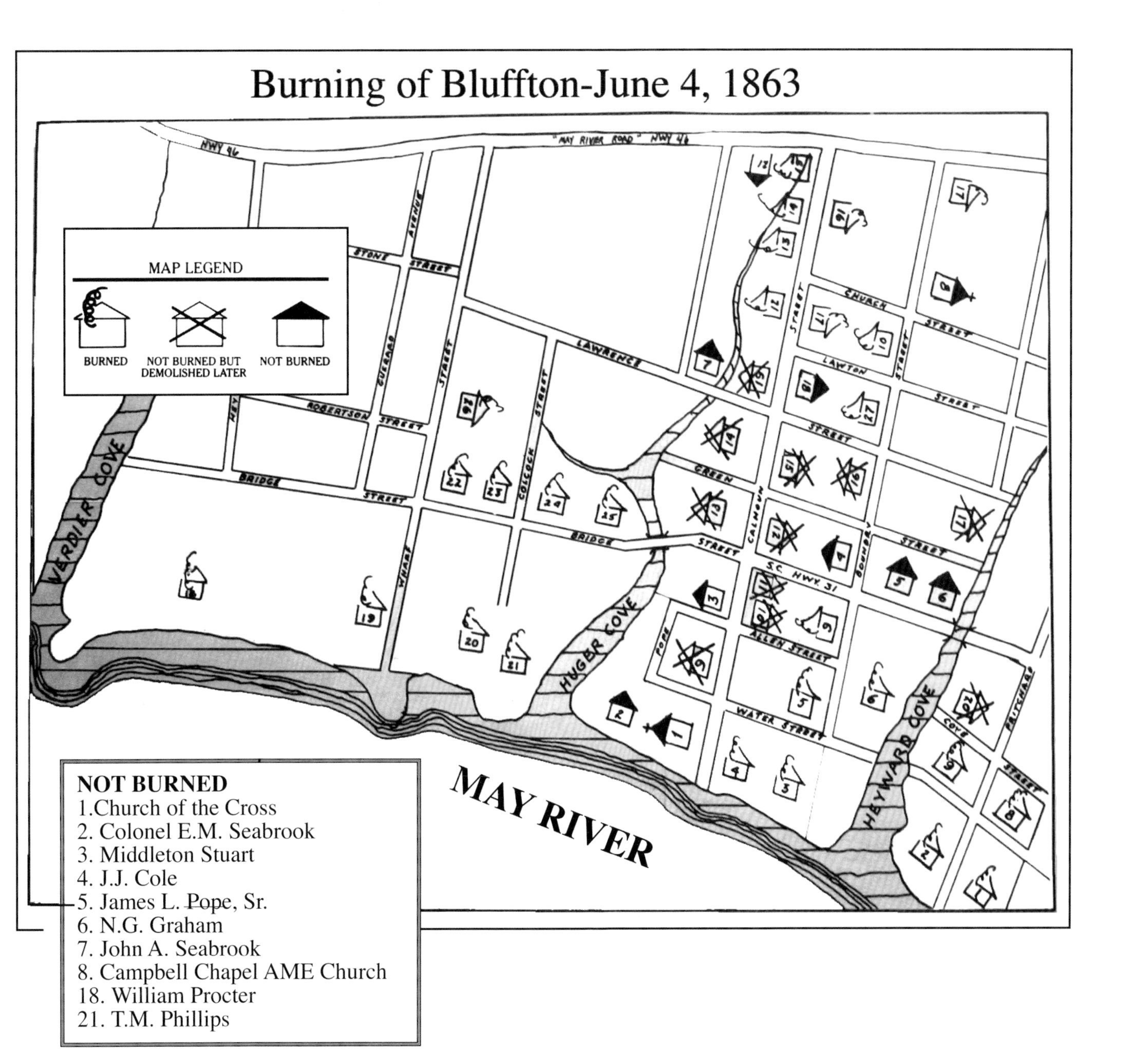
Burning of Bluffton-June 4, 1863
MAP LEGEND
BURNED
NOT BURNED BUT DEMOLISHED LATER
NOT BURNED
"MAY RIVER ROAD" HWY 46
HWY 46
STONE STREET
AVENUE
GUERARD
ROBERTSON STREET
BRIDGE STREET
WHARF
COLCOCK STREET
LAWRENCE
GREEN
BRIDGE STREET
CALHOUN
S.C. HWY. 31
BOUNDRY
ALLEN STREET
POPE
WATER STREET
CHURCH STREET
LAWTON STREET
STREET
COVE STREET
PRITCHARD
VERDIER COVE
HUGER COVE
HEYWARD COVE
MAY RIVER
NOT BURNED
1.Church of the Cross
2. Colonel E.M. Seabrook
3. Middleton Stuart
4. J.J. Cole
5. James L. Pope, Sr.
6. N.G. Graham
7. John A. Seabrook
8. Campbell Chapel AME Church
18. William Procter
21. T.M. Phillips

When the Union
soldiers burned
Bluffton during
the Civil War
they were ordered
not to destroy
this old Episcopal
church, which
still stands on
the bluff.
D. M.
March 1907
BLUFFTON
S. C.

SOUTH TOUR

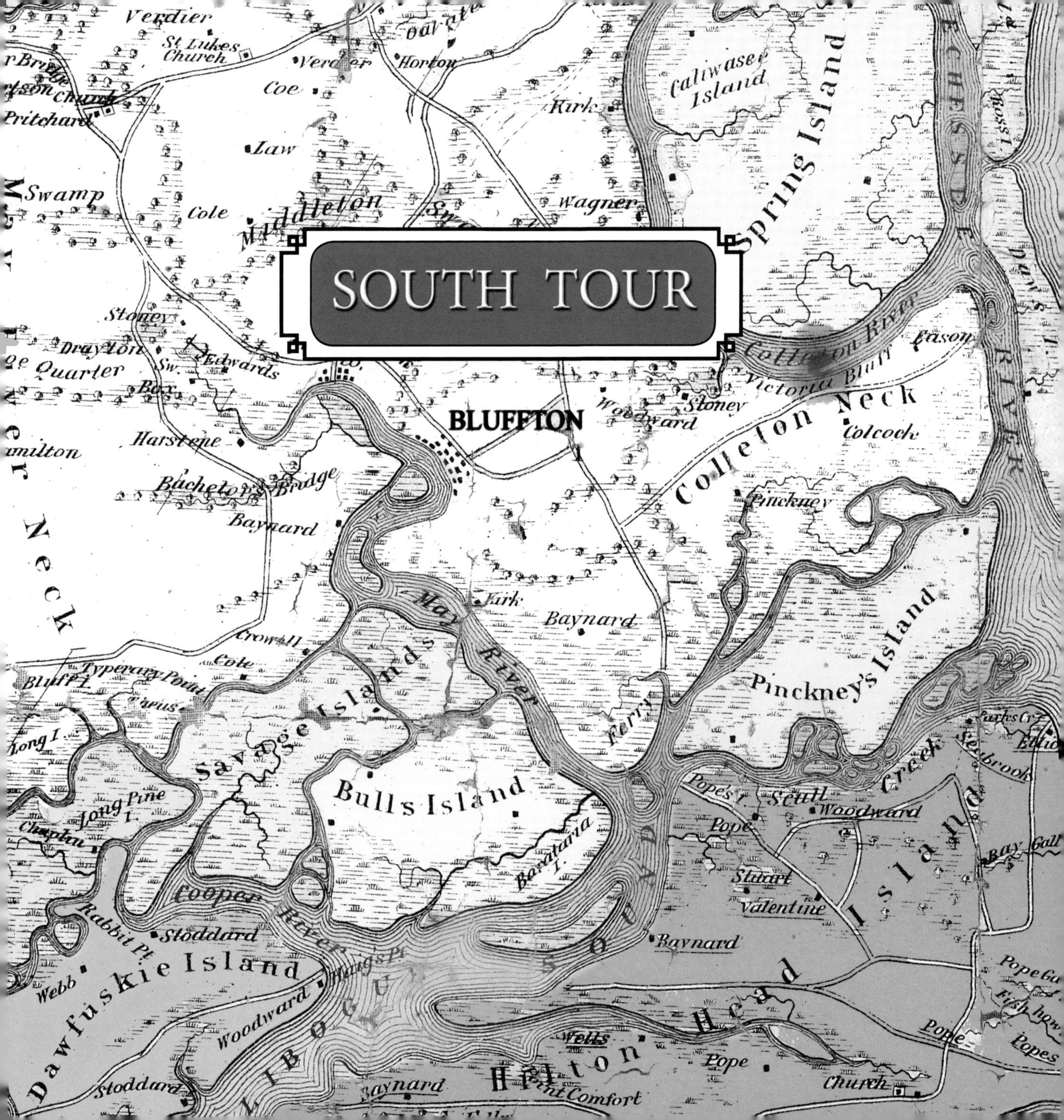

BLUFFTON

Verdier
St Lukes Church
Verdier
Horton
Bridge
Church
Pritchard
Coe
Kirk
Caliwasee Island
Spring Island
Law
Swamp
Cole
Middleton
Wagner
Stoney
Drayton
Quarter
Sw.
Edwards
Box
Colleton River
Victoria Bluff
Eason
Stoney
Woodward
Colleton Neck
Colcock
Harstene
Hamilton
Bachelors Bridge
Baynard
Colleton
Pinckney
May River Neck
Kirk
May River
Baynard
Crowell
Cole
Typerary Point
Bluff I.
Savage Islands
Pinckney's Island
Ferry
Long I.
Bulls Island
Long Pine I.
Chaplin
Barataria I.
Popes
Scull Creek
Seabrook
Woodward
Pope
Stuart
Valentine
Cooper River
Rabbit Pt
Stoddard
Baynard
Dawfuskie Island
Webb
Haigs Pt
Woodward
Calibogue Sound
Hilton Head Island
Wells
Pope
Church
Stoddard
Baynard
Point Comfort
Pope
Popes
Chechessee River

No. 1. THE COLE-HEYWARD HOUSE, c. 1840
70 Boundary Street
HEYWARD HOUSE HISTORIC CENTER (HHHC)
WELCOME CENTER, TOWN OF BLUFFTON

Slave Quarters

This house is an outstanding example of an early Carolina Farmhouse style brought to North America by planters from the West Indies. The earliest part of the house, the north parlor and bedroom above, were built by John J. Cole and his slaves in the early 1840s as a summer home for his wife Caroline Corley and their children. [He was a planter who owned Moreland Plantation located on present day Palmetto Bluff.] It's possible that the recently restored slave cabin was built first to house the construction crew. By 1860, Cole had more than doubled the size of the house and his family, at which time the front and side windows in the front rooms were much enlarged. Nothing went to waste and the original parlor windows were reused in the dining room and back bedroom. The interior is clad with wide heart pine boards. Over and under fireplaces warmed the house on both stories where 3 original mantels may be seen.

The original unattached summer kitchen [which may have stood near the northwest corner of the original house] was pulled down and replaced by a large square attached kitchen in the 1930s. Boards from the summer kitchen were probably used to construct the small garage.

Following the Civil War, Mr. Cole who had contracted tuberculosis during his service, died. The Cole family, their fortune wiped out, sold their holdings in Bluffton and moved to Texas in 1874. Mrs. Kate Du Bois, wife of the Federally appointed Post Master, purchased the property [and many others in Bluffton] then sold it in 1882 to Mrs. George Cuthbert Heyward, Sr. and it remained in the Heyward family until its purchase in 1998 by the Bluffton Historical Preservation Society. It is now preserved and open to the public as the town's only house museum and has been designated the official welcome center for the Town of Bluffton.

From the Heyward House, cross Bridge St. and continue south on Boundary for the South Tour.

No. 2. THE RATE, c. 1948
Corner of Bridge and Boundary Streets

Art work courtesy of Christina Bates

This small structure, built by Galliard Heyward as a store on his property served as an ice cream and tobacco shop and also as a post office.

Continue south on Boundary Street

No. 3. THE GUILFORD HOUSE, c. 1921
82 Boundary Street

No. 4. THE CANTRELL HOUSE, c.1940
84 Boundary Street.

No. 5. THE PINE HOUSE, c. 1904-1905
95 Boundary Street

Photo - Thomas Heyward

This beautifully wooded site was the home of General Thomas Ferguson Drayton, of Civil War fame, [burned on 4 June 1863]. It was later purchased by Dr. Hammond Eve who built a home on the property facing Heyward Cove. The property was sold in 1902 to Dr. Freeman Valentine Walker and his wife Mary McAlpin of Savannah, GA. That house burned in 1904 and the Walkers built the Pine House which was finished 20 February 1905 as attested by the cornerstone. The contractor-carpenter was Nathan Crosby, a member of a pioneer Bluffton family.

The exterior of the house was finished with pine shingles, reminiscent of the New England shoreline where Dr. Walker was raised. Screened porches graced the north and south facades. The original interior had large rooms with 13' high ceilings, wide pine plank flooring and paneled walls, and an unusual feature for Bluffton, a rue basement about 14' x 14'.

The late Mr. & Mrs. Gaillard S. Heyward, [she was Postmistress from 1953-75] bought the property from Mrs. Walker's estate in 1943. Thomas Heyward began alterations of this house in 2006. Photo of the Pine House courtesy of Thomas Heyward.

Continue south on Boundary to Water Street and turn right onto Water

No. 6. THE WHITNEY COTTAGE, c. 1910
10 Water Street

This lovely one-story frame weatherboard dwelling built in a Lowcountry vernacular form was constructed by Frank Whitney c. 1910 as a guest cottage. It provided additional rooms for visitors to the Lawton House, a boarding house that was on the same property. The cottage has a gable-on-hip roof, and a shed roof porch supported by columns with a simple balustrade.

Continue west on Water Street and left on Calhoun Street

No. 7. THE SQUIRE POPE CARRIAGE HOUSE, c. 1850 (JOINED 1865)
111 Calhoun Street

Originally serving as the carriage house and outbuildings for the summer house of Squire William Pope, this two-story frame structure, circa 1850 is located at the back of a deep lot overlooking the May River. Pope was a wealthy landowner from Hilton Head Island [owner of Coggins Point Plantation]. He served in the South Carolina Senate and represented St. Luke's Parrish in the SC House of Representatives. The main house was burned the day of the firing of Bluffton. When the family returned following the Civil War, they joined these buildings together to serve as their home. The structure is one room deep with porches across the river façade.

No. 8. OLD TOWN WHARF PAVILION, c. 1920
Southern end of Calhoun Street

From Bluffton's earliest days, commercial activity centered on this area where a wharf for docking packet boats and steamers laden with passengers, mail and commercial goods unloaded. The local plantation products: rice, cotton, indigo and naval stores were thence shipped to the regional ports of Savannah and Charleston for sale by factors dealing in goods bound for northern US and European buyers. Local farm produce was probably sold at the famous Savannah Market building on Barnard Street.

Sometime in the 20th C., a Pavilion was built across the end of the wharf, and many a community gathering was held there including dances.

Reverse course and go north on Calhoun Street.

No. 9. THE CHURCH OF THE CROSS, c. 1854 or 1857
110 Calhoun Street

This handsome Gothic revival style structure was designed by the Charleston architect Edward Brickell White, who, circa 1853 accepted the contract to build the church to seat five to six hundred parishioners at a cost of $5,000. Construction started in 1854 and culminated with first services being held July 17, 1857. [This new church located on the bluff overlooking the May River replaced the small Episcopal Chapel of the Cross located on the southeast corner of Calhoun and Bridge streets.] Reverend James Stoney was the Rector.

Constructed entirely of heart of long leaf pine on brick piers, the exterior siding is of board and batten; lancet shaped windows display unusual "palmetto frond" shutter panels that fill the tops, and louvered center opening shutters. Inside, the windows, containing some of the original pink glass from England open to the interior to allow excellent cross ventilation. The cruciform interior shows balconies in each transcept over boxed pews and the impressive open cross-timbered roof and more boxed pews in the nave. The walls are pink plaster scored to look like large building blocks. A bell tower was added to the north entrance in 1878 when the bell was returned to the church, having been found at the Porter School in Charleston. At one time in this "summer colony", the winter services were held in the narthex, due to the small off-season congregation; heat was provided by a pot bellied stove. Original lighting was provided by whale oil or kerosene chandeliers and sconces.

This church was placed on the National Register of Historic Places in 1975.

Turn left on Water Street, and view the front of the Allen-Lockwood House on your right.

No. 10. THE ALLEN-LOCKWOOD HOUSE, c. 1850
94 Calhoun Street

This cottage was built by William Gaston Allen on the northwest corner of Calhoun and Water Streets in the early 1850s for his wife Susan Virginia Bolan and their six children. It is a classic example of a Lowcountry summer cottage with its gabled roof, commodious high-ceilinged rooms and numerous windows for cross-ventilation. Raised on brick piers, a wide porch spans the south façade.

Colonel Allen was a prosperous planter of the May River Neck area, but by 1866, he was bankrupt. At a forced sale in 1873, his daughter, Susan Virginia [Mrs. Thomas Postell Lockwood] bought the house for $10; it remained in the family until 1953.

Continue west on Water Street

No. 11. THE HUGER-GORDON HOUSE, c. 1850
9 Water Street

Huger Yard illustration by Naomi McCracken

This is the only antebellum house located on the bluff overlooking the May River that survived the Federal firing of Bluffton [4 June 1863]. Minnie balls, lodged in the front door studs give evidence of the sniping that took place between Federal forces and Confederate pickets here.

The frame one and a half story building is placed on a low brick foundation of piers with a gabled roof and interior chimneys. A one story veranda with a shed roof and chamfered posts, runs the width of the house on the riverside and the central dormer has glass doors cut into the eave of the roof and veranda. It is believed the house was built around 1795 and enlarged in the 1820s.

The owner in 1863 was Colonel Ephraim Mikell Seabrook who had acquired the property from Dr. William Lowndes Hamilton in 1855. Dr. Joseph Alston Huger, II bought the property from the Seabrook's in 1882 and it has remained in the Huger family. Mr. & Mrs. Hugh Gordon made alterations to the exterior and interior in the 1970s.

Turn right on Pope Street and turn right on Allen Street toward Calhoun Street

No. 12. SEVEN OAKS, c. 1850
82 Calhoun Street

This is presently a two-story raised house with double verandas on the south and east sides and two exterior chimneys. Part of it was built about 1850. According to a story, it is called Seven Oaks due to seven very large live oak stumps that support the house. Some of the original interior details remain; there is a visible line running east to west down the center of the northeast parlor floor, indicating that an addition was made at some time.

The first owner of the house was Colonel Middleton Stuart and his wife, Emma Barnwell Stoney. In 1866 the property was sold to Frances Marion Edward; subsequently, it was owned by Ephraim Mikell Baynard, then E. J. Harrison and later by the Baynard family of Hilton Head Island.

In the 1920s, Mrs. Elizabeth Sanders operated Seven Oaks as a popular and successful boarding house for salesmen and summer visitors.

Pass the side of Seven Oaks and turn left on Calhoun Street

Antique postcard showing the c.1890 Methodist Church built under the leadership of the Reverend W. R. Buchanan. In 1940 a hurricane blew a tree down into the roof of the sanctuary causing most of the structure to be demolished. It was later replaced with the present Methodist church on the same site.

No. 13. THE GRAVES HOUSE, c. 1915
85 Calhoun Street

George Sewell Guilford of Portland, Maine was a ship's carpenter and while in Liverpool, England he met and married Jane Hore. He brought his bride to the states, and after homesteading in Florida they moved to Scotia, South Carolina and then to Bluffton. Guilford built the Graves House about 1915 for his daughter Cora Jane and her husband John S. Graves, Sr. and they raised their family here.

The house has a distinctive four-gabled roof line that gives it a strong New England flavor reminiscent of the builder's Yankee heritage, but showing the same foundation, [built on raised piers] and wide porches to allow the optimum convection in the days before electricity and air conditioning.

Continue north on Calhoun Street

No. 14. THE FRIPP-LOWDEN HOUSE, c. 1909
80 Calhoun Street

This Lowcountry cottage was built in 1909, (also by Nathan Crosby) for Alfred Fripp and his wife Sallie Williams. A fine small house, it is a one-story frame building of pine with a porch across the façade. It is surrounded by a garden started by Mrs. Fripp who raised camellias. "The Sallie Fripp" can be seen here when in bloom and is a favorite in many Bluffton gardens. The Fripp's daughter Mrs. H. O. Lowden, Jr. continued to expand the garden.

Today, The Hank McCrackens have restored the house and gardens and added a wrought iron fence and garage.

In 1915, Mr. Fripp erected a store on the corner of the property at Calhoun and Bridge streets and sold general merchandise of all varieties. That building was damaged by an out-of-control car and demolished in 1980, (see photo at right)

From the intersection of Calhoun and Bridge Streets, continue north on Calhoun Street for the North Tour

Looking North on Calhoun Street c. 1900

From the intersection of Calhoun and Bridge Streets, continue North on Calhoun St. for the North Tour

NORTH TOUR

BLUFFTON

St Lukes Church
Verdier
Horton
Coe
Kirk
Caliwase Island
Spring Island
Law
Swamp
Cole
Middleton
Wagner
Stoney
Drayton
Quarter
Edwards
Box
Colleton River
Victoria Bluff
Eason
Woodward
Stoney
Colleton Neck
Colcock
Harstene
amilton
Bachelors Bridge
Baynard
Pinckney
River Neck
Kirk
May River
Baynard
Crowell
Cole
Typerary Point
Bluff I.
Savage Islands
Pinckney's Island
Ferry
Long I.
Bulls Island
Long Pine I.
Chaplin
Barataria I.
Pope's I.
Scull Creek
Woodward
Seabrook
Pope
Stuart
Valentine
Cooper River
Rabbit Pt.
Stoddard
Baynard
Dawfuskie Island
Webb
Haigs Pt.
Woodward
Calibogue Sound
Hilton Head Island
Wells
Pope
Stoddard
Baynard
Point Comfort
Church
Pope
Popes
Fish haul
Bay Gall
Parks Cr.
Elliott
Pope Gall
Dawss I.
Ross I.
Echessee River

No. 15. THE STORE, c. 1904
56 Calhoun Street

The Store sits on a tract, bounded by Calhoun St. on the east, Green St. on the south, Lawrence St. on the north and Huger Cove on the west, which is thought to have been the property of Mrs. John Hais Hardee, nee Harriet Saussy. She was listed as the "Head of the Household" and a "Planter" in both the 1850 and 1860 Census. There are no known records of who owned the property from 1865 to 1900 when it was owned briefly by the Trustees of school district #2. In 1904, Jesse Davidore Peeples of Scotia, SC bought the property and built a store and a commodious home beside it for his family. He had five children by his first wife, Willie Mae Stokes and ten by his second wife, Maud Estella Guilford. The house [now falling down] contained six bedrooms and a large sleeping porch.

The Peeples House

The Store, until the late 1990s was a one story structure surmounted by a high gable roof and with flanking enclosed side wings with shed roofs. The double front doors which have glass panels in the transom, open under a shed roof front porch supported by four square posts.

Turn left onto Lawrence Street and view the side of the Mulligan House.

No 16. THE MULLIGAN HOUSE, c. 1948
44 Calhoun Street

No. 17. THE DISPENSARY SITE, c. 1855
Lawrence Street (Probably located west of the Mulligan House.)

Built by the DuBois family as a shop for medicines and other household necessaries, it was a log structure.

Continue west on Lawrence to the Seabrook House.

No. 18. THE SEABROOK HOUSE, c. 1850
47 Lawrence Street

Built in the 1840-50s, this is a typical Low-country house, a two-story frame weatherboard structure sits on six foot high brick piers. There are two dormer windows on the north and south sides of a steeply pitched gabled roof. On the north side are two very tall brick chimneys. The kitchen may be the old summer kitchen raised on piers and attached to the house during the 20th C.

John Archibald Seabrook is believed to have been the original owner. He owned Foot Point plantation and was also an assistant minister at the Chapel of the Cross in the 1850s. In 1876 the property was sold to Egbert and Kate H. Du Bois of Dutchess County, NY. He had been made postmaster of Bluffton following the Civil War.

The house was purchased and carefully restored in 2000 by Mr. & Mrs. Van DuBose who won the BHPS Caldwell Award for Historic Preservation.

Return to Calhoun Street, turn left. Follow the Tour along the west (left side) of Calhoun and when you get to May River Road, continue the Tour along the east side of Calhoun.

No. 19. THE CARSON COTTAGE, c. 1890
38 Calhoun Street

J. J. Carson distinguished himself at the Battle of Chancellorsville, May 2-4, 1863, by braving the gunfire of the battleground and rescuing the mortally wounded General Stonewall Jackson. Placing Jackson's body in a buckboard, Carson drove back through enemy lines to the Confederate's side. After the Civil War, he returned to Bluffton and built the cottage about 1890. Here in 1900, he organized the First Baptist Church of Bluffton and services were held in the house until a church building was completed.

This one-story house on short piers has a charming front porch. The structure was recently moved forward and renovated.

No. 20. THE D. HASELL HEYWARD HOUSE, c. 1914
32 Calhoun Street

This fine example of a Lowcountry cottage was built by Nathan Crosby in 1914 for Daniel Hasell Heyward, Sr. and his wife Hattie Mae Mulligan. Constructed of pine on high brick pilings it has a wide central hallway flanked by large high-ceilinged rooms with horizontal narrow pine boards on the walls and ceilings, simple moldings and tall windows front and back. A wide porch stretches the length of the front façade.

The structure was carefully restored by Lewis Hammett, Jr. Esq. and serves as his law offices.

No. 21. THE PATZ BROTHERS HOUSE, c. 1892
26 Calhoun Street

The history of these houses and the Planters Mercantile are woven together. The Patz brothers, Moses and Abram, came from the northeast, possibly New York State, circa 1890. They built the Mercantile first [probably living above the store] and then in 1892 constructed a semi-detached double residence next door. The paired houses were mirror images with highly decorative eave and porch ornamentation of the late Victorian age. This style, rare in other parts of the country is very prevalent in the south. However, it is the only one of two of its kind in Bluffton. The houses share a central wall, while each house had its own front door, hall, stairway and six rooms. It has been said that the wives feuded and did not speak to each other for many years.

Mr. & Mrs. Lewis J. Hammett, Jr. restored the exterior, removed the interior dividing wall to allow for a wide handsome central staircase leading to the upstairs.

No. 22. THE PLANTERS MERCANTILE, c. 1890
20 Calhoun Street

Unlike most 19th C. commercial buildings on Calhoun St., the Mercantile is built with two full stories; the ground floor store has very high ceilings, tall windows and entry doors. The store was a thriving business, called affectionately by owners and patrons alike, "The Jew Store", which offered the area, according to their billhead: Clothing, Dry Goods, Boots, Shoes, Hats and Groceries, Furniture, Wagons, Buggies and Harness, Sewing Machines, Trunks and Satchels, Cigars, Feed, etc., Grits and Flour A Specialty, Boat Supplies, Coffins and Fixture.

Abram suffered an untimely death; [it is said that he awoke in the middle of the night with a stomach ache and went next door to the store to find something to relieve his pain. In the dark he poured a dollop of carbolic acid, gulped it down and was found dead the next morning]. In 1920 Moses sold the entire property to Julius Ulman and J. Weitz; then in 1930 Paul J. Viens bought it. It then passed back and forth between the Viens and the Pinckneys, during which time a Mr. Goodman operated a store there. After his death, Morris Robinowich kept store there until 1972. Many illustrious individuals and groups have operated shops and stores therein.

No. 23. THE CORDRAY HOUSE, c. 1910
1 Calhoun Street

In the 1860 Census for St. Luke's Parish, one Isaac H. Martin, mason, a free black, his wife Pauline H. Martin and their children, Philip, Mary E., Isiah and John H. are listed as living in the block bounded on the north by May River Road (now Hwy. 46), west by Calhoun St., east by Boundary St. and south by Church St. In the Charleston Mercury account of the 1863 firing of Bluffton, it is stated that the Federal Troops set fire to the Martin House [as well as many houses and other structures in the Town].

The 1913 Plat Map of the Town of Bluffton shows the Martin property had been divided into several lots, including the site of the present Cordray House. Several families have owned parts of this property.

The last remaining Praise House [built to house a new congregation while money was obtained to build a full size church] in the Historic District is behind the Cordray House.

Return to Calhoun Street and continue the tour on the east side of the street. Turn left on Church Street.

No. 24. OLD BLUFFTON TABERNACLE, moved c. 1935
10 Church Street

Now the pottery studio and gallery of Jacob Preston, this structure was originally a Baptist church, and like many of Bluffton's historic treasures, is an "Artifact of Poverty", according to Jacob Preston who discovered that many parts of it were recycled from other buildings: tin roof, and various sized windows came from other structures and the wiring was essentially lamp cord.

Return to Calhoun Street.

No. 25. THE COASTAL BATTERY HOUSING, c. 1940
27& 29 Calhoun St.

These military housing structures were moved from Hilton Head Island to Bluffton, sometime after WW II, by barge, possibly by Paul Pinckney, to replace housing lost in 1863. Since then, they have served as homes, medical offices, retail stores and art galleries.

Housing illustration by Naomi McCracken

As Naomi McCracken's illustrations demonstrare, Bluffton was not a town of mansions but rather a village of cottages on narrow deep lots, small commercial structures and churches.

Continue to the intersection of Calhoun and Bridge Streets and turn left onto Bridge Street and after passing the Heyward House, cross Boundary Street for the East Tour.

EAST TOUR

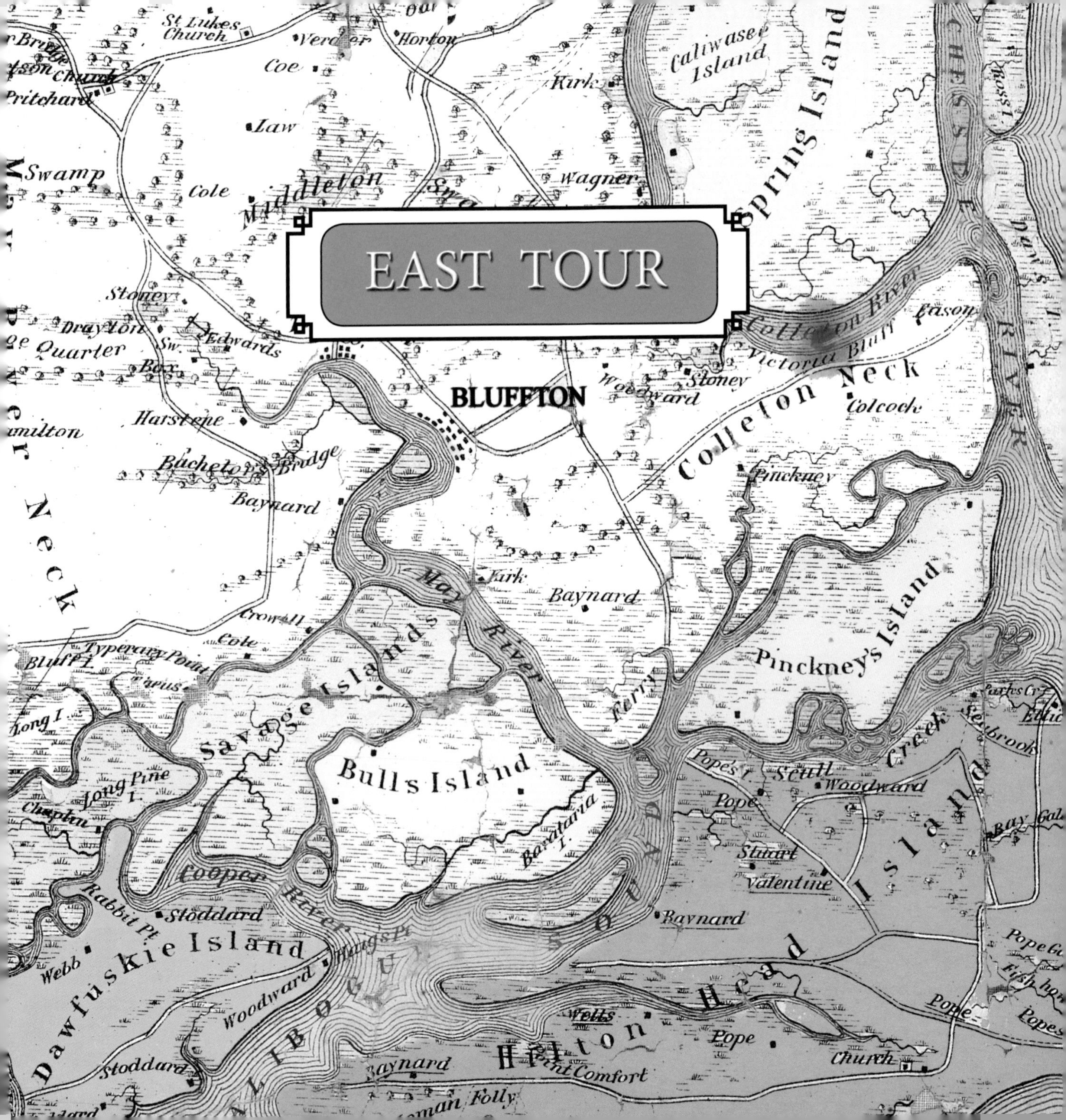
BLUFFTON
St Lukes Church
Coe
Horton
Law
Kirk
Cole
Swamp
Middleton
Wagner
Caliwasse Island
Spring Island
Stoney
Drayton
Quarter
Edwards
Box
Harstene
Buckelow's Bridge
Baynard
Colleton River
Victoria Bluff
Eason
Colleton Neck
Colcock
Stoney
Woodward
Pinckney
May River
Kirk
Baynard
Crowell
Cole
Typerary Point
Bluff I.
Long I.
Savage Islands
Pinckney's Island
Ferry
Bulls Island
Long Pine I.
Chaplin
Barataria I.
Pope's I.
Scull Creek
Woodward
Seabrook
Pope
Stuart
Valentine
Baynard
Cooper River
Rabbit Pt.
Stoddard
Webb
Dawfuskie Island
Haigs Pt.
Woodward
Calibogue Sound
Hilton Head Island
Wells
Pope
Church
Point Comfort
Baynard
Stoddard
Pope
Chester River
Ross I.
May River Neck

No. 26. The FRIPP HOUSE, c. 1835
48 Bridge St.

This two story wood frame house was constructed using a central hall floor plan on eight foot high piers, making it the only one of its kind in town; it is believed to have been built circa 1835 by James L. Pope. Late in the 20th C. the raised basement was enclosed. The house has clapboard siding and 3 external chimneys. The second story front porch was originally used as a sleeping porch. The earliest records known show the property was owned by Pope prior to 1847. He died in 1863 and the property was inherited by his son Dr. James L. Pope, Jr. It remained in the family until 1883 when his widow sold it to Rebecca N. Sams. In 1885, Mr. & Mrs. William J. Fripp purchased it, owning it until 1919. Since that time, several later 20th C. owners have made various alterations and additions and sold off part of the property.

No. 27. The CARD HOUSE, c. 1825
34 Bridge St.

The origin of this simple antebellum home is difficult to document; it is believed to be the oldest remaining residence in Bluffton. Undocumented sources indicate the house was built circa 1825. The first owner of record is William J. Graham who owned it in 1847. Another deed shows the property was owned by Sarah G. Norton. A 1913 survey map shows that the land was then owned by the Fripp family. The two-story section centers flanking shed roof wings. Entry from the front porch gives directly into the present living room with a large fireplace. On the north side of the fireplace was the original closet spiral staircase to the second floor. The original house was one room deep, a two story block flanked by shed roof wings. The most likely story associated with the unusual name of this house is that in the 1840s during a high stake poker session held in the house, William Eddings Baynard won the deed to the 1,000 acre Braddock's Point plantation on Hilton Head Island from the unfortunate owner John Stoney.

Continue East on Bridge Street.

No. 28. HEYWARD COVE BRIDGE

Heyward Cove is one of four major coves off the May River cutting from SW to NE through the town. They bring waterfront views and breezes deep into the historic district and are treasured for their benefits. During the 19th C., skids were built over the coves to provide access for pedestrians walking east and west on Water Street.

Cross the bridge and continue East on Bridge Street, turn right on Prichard Street, (sign is misspelled).

No. 29. The BLUFF, c. 1883
130 Prichard St.

A large area along the May River was owned by James Kirk, Sr. and called Kirk's Bluff. His daughter, Mary Agnes married Colonel Joseph J. Stoney and they built a house at this location [burned 4 June 1863]. In 1883, John Guerard Heyward purchased the lot and built a two-story house. The second story was swept away by the hurricane of 1893 and was never replaced. Remaining is a one-story frame house with weatherboard exterior and three brick chimneys – one interior and two exterior; the house is still heated with wood fires. A full width river facing front porch has been partially filled in to create a bedroom. The property transferred between various Heyward family members until 1921 when George Cuthbert Heyward, Jr. acquired it. The Bluff was used as a summer home by the Heywards, who lived in Savannah, until Mr. Heyward's retirement when the family moved to Bluffton permanently. The appearance of the house is much changed to make it a comfortable year-round home.

No. 30. PRICHARD ST. PARK, 2001
View the May River and read Bluffton's Covenant. (The Prichard St. park sits between the Prichard House and The Bluff.).

No. 31 The PRICHARD HOUSE, 1890 & Guest House, c. 1905
131 Prichard St.

Dr. Paul Fitzsimons Prichard, who was a successful rice planter, physician and signer of the petition to charter the Town of Bluffton built a summer house [date unknown] for his wife Martha Catherine Kirk, at this location overlooking the May River. The house, burned during the firing of Bluffton, was probably sited on what is now the front lawn, surrounded by many old live oak trees. In the mid 1890s, Charles Teft Prichard, one of their sons, built a Queen Anne Victorian house sited further back from but facing the river with unusual architectural details to suit the climate. Not only was the house raised on piers, with a deep porch facing the south onto which four tall windows could be raised into the wall providing direct access, but the north side of the house was wider than the front by four and one-half feet on each side to catch the prevailing south west breezes which could pass freely through small rooms with 12 foot ceilings. In 1904, Charles died leaving his widow Agnes (Kearney) and five small children in financial difficulty. She built a pine guest house with three bedrooms, each opening onto a deep front porch that faced west on the property line by the river. [Plumbing, until the 1940s was a privy hung over the bluff] and took in boarders, mainly school teachers and summer visitors.

ST.JOHN'S BAPTIST CHURCH, demolished

Return to Bridge Street and continue going north on Prichard Steet.

No. 32. OLD ONE ROOM SCHOOL HOUSE, c.1910
60 Prichard St.

Continue down Prichard Street to Bruin Road, turn left.

No. 33 JULIA JOYNER KING COTTAGE, c. 1945
16 Bruin Rd.

No. 34 OLD BRUIN COTTAGE, c.1945
6 Bruin Rd.

No. 35 JOYNER HOUSE, c.1940
7 Bruin Rd.

Turn left onto Boundary Street.

36.CAMPBELL CHAPEL AME CHURCH, c. 1853
23 Boundary St.

Serving today as a secondary building for the African Methodist Episcopal Church, this building was constructed by the Methodist Episcopal Church in 1853 under the leadership of Reverend George Allen. The design is of the Greek revival style, temple form, with the exterior clad in board and batten siding, many tall windows and four square columns supporting the pedimented front gable. It was fire damaged by the infamous burning of Bluffton, but was not destroyed.

In 1874, the few remaining members of the congregation voted to sell the structure to the African Methodist Episcopal Church members. Additions and alterations were made in 1969.

37. BOARD AND BATTEN HOUSE, c. 1880
43 Boundary St.

There are only two examples of two-family houses in town. History tells many interesting stories about the use of this structure! Made of heart pine with a shared chimney.

The Reverend Louis "Bubsy" Graham and his wife lived here. He was the Reverend at St. John's Church and some say if you were walking by on a Saturday night you might hear him practicing his Sunday sermon. The house was built around 1900.

No. 38. CALDWELL ARCHIVE – BHPS
48 Boundary St.

Insets from 1757 deBrahm map

Caldwell Archives: in 2005 the town leased the old library building at 48 Boundary St. to BHPS and the Archives (now called the Caldwell Archive) was moved to part of the building. The archives continue to add historical and current papers, photographs, maps, and documents to its collection and is open by appointment for anyone interested in looking for information.

Turn right on Lawrence Street.

No. 39. BEECH HOUSE, c. 1930
65 Lawrence St.

The Beech House was purchased by "Kiss" Beech. Recently restored by Michael Hahn, and painted white with high contrast shutters and other details.

Return to Calhoun Street and turn left to the intersection of Bridge and Calhoun for the start of the West Tour.

Filling Station c.1915 formerly across from The Store on Calhoun Street

WEST TOUR

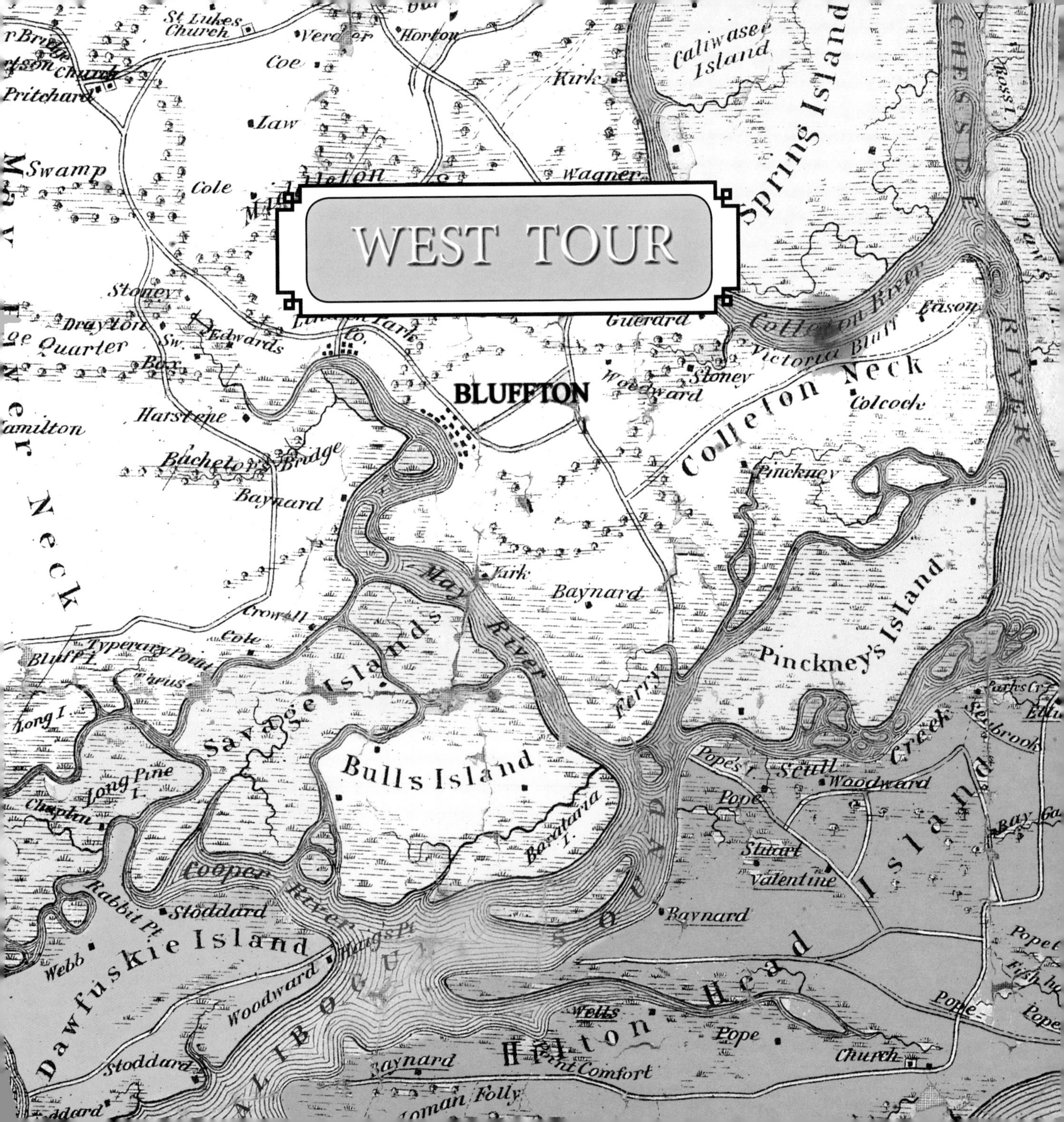

BLUFFTON

St Lukes Church
Verdier
Horton
Caliwasee Island
Spring Island
Coe
Kirk
Pritchard
Law
Swamp
Cole
Wagner
Stoney
Drayton
Edwards
Quarter
Box
Guerard
Colleton River
Victoria Bluff
Eason
Stoney
Woodward
Colleton Neck
Colcock
Harstene
Bachelors Bridge
Baynard
Pinckney
Hamilton
May River Neck
Jark
Baynard
May River
Crowell
Cole
Typerary Point
Bluff P.
Savage Islands
Ferry
Pinckney's Island
Long I.
Long Pine I.
Chaplin
Bulls Island
Barataria I.
Pope's I.
Scull
Woodward
Pope
Creek
Seabrook
Stuart
Valentine
Cooper River
Rabbit Pt.
Stoddard
Baynard
Dawfuskie Island
Webb
Hunts Pt.
Woodward
Calibogue Sound
Hilton Head Island
Wells
Pope
Church
Pope
Stoddard
Baynard
Point Comfort
Folly
Chesesssee River

40. SARAH RILEY HOOKS COTTAGE, c. 1920
70 Bridge Street

This was known as the Michael C. Riley House. His daughter, Sara Riley Hooks was born on the property in 1922. Michael was known as "Mikey" and was a believer in education. He was appointed to the Board of Education after WWII. During this time a new school was built in Bluffton on Goethe Road and was named in his honor. This building was demolished in 1990 and a new school was built on Burnt Church Road and kept the same name, Michael C. Riley Elementary School.

Sara Riley Hooks remained in Bluffton and worked as a home health care nurse and lived in the family home,where she was born, until her death.

Turn left on Colcock Street.

41. COLCOCK-TEEL HOUSE, c. 1890
46 Colcock Street

Francis Horton Colcock, fifth South Carolina generation descendant of John Colcock of England, was born in 1855 in Huntsville, Alabama. A graduate of Porter Military and Union College, he studied law and was admitted to the South Carolina bar. He also had a degree in Civil Engineering and was a professor of mathematics at the University of South Carolina in Columbia.

Having strong family ties to Bluffton, he built this summer home in 1890 for his wife, Mary Robert Jones and their four children. The house has open porches on the south and west sides and is finished outside with heart pine clapboard, painted gray with white trim and black shutters.

After his death in 1925, the property was inherited by his daughter Frances Horton Colcock, who married Leslie Marmaduke Teel of Garvin, Oklahoma, and has remained in the Teel family.

42. CEDAR BLUFF, c.1890
51 Colcock Street

The first owner of the Cedar Bluff property may have been Captain William Pope. However the first owner of record was Richard Richardson Pope who built his summer home there on the bluff in the 1840s [burned 4 June 1863]. His son, James Franklin Pope, Jr. sold the property to the Thomas Rhett Heyward [Eugenia Coe] family who built the present house. All the windows, doors, transoms, blinds, sashes etc. were purchased for $143.00 from Andrew Manley in Savannah and shipped to Bluffton.

The house is described in the LSH II as being of late Victorian style, with a large central hall and half octagon wings on either side [it is rumored that the second floor was used as a ballroom by the Heywards]. Eugenia Coe Heyward sold the property in 1921 to David C. Barrow of Savannah.

In the late 1930s, Mr. and Mrs. Samuels owned it and operated a restaurant called "The Silver Eagle" renowned for its delicious Lowcountry cuisine.

In 1961 Ralph Grady Hill, then owner sold the property to Mrs. Lawrence Blun Dunn [Mary Strachan] of Savannah for their summer home. The property remains in the family.

Return to Bridge Street and turn left.

43. ORAGE COTTAGE,c. 1930 
92 Bridge Street

Named for its first occupants, the Orage cottage was originally constructed in the 1930s. Restoration and renovation, begun in May of 2001 exposed the original pine lap siding and exposed rafter tails that are common characteristics of shot gun form architecture. The interior bead board ceilings and pine floors were also restored. Having extensive termite damage, the front porch was demolished and replaced by a large open-air porch and a rear façade addition added. The owners received the Caldwell Award for Historic Preservation in 2002.

Turn left on Wharf Street.

44. BLUFFTON OYSTER FACTORY, c. 1940
63 Wharf Street

This building and operation represents the last commercial fresh oyster shucking house on the East Coast of the U.S. It is the 4th oldest continuously operating business in the State of South Carolina. The current building constructed in 1940 replaced an earlier board and batten factory building with a large boiler used in the canning process. This one story structure has a raised seam metal gabled roof and a partial width shed roof porch.

Garvey House, c. 1865
Town of Bluffton, Oyster Factory Park

Also within what is now a town park and boat landing area is the only known freedman's cottage built on the waterfront. What remains of Mr. Garvey's house (shown here in an early photo) stands on the West side of Wharf Street within the park. It was originally a one and one-half story, three bay wide structure on brick piers with weatherboard siding and fronted by a porch supported by six square columns. A single chimney stood on the west end and the windows were six over six lights with center opening shutters.

Return to Bridge Street and turn left.

45. THE HANCOCK-MINOR HOUSE, c. 1939
111 Bridge Street

This house was built in the late 1930s by Jim Hancock.

46. THE TYSON-DERST COTTAGE, c. 1939
113 Bridge Street

Enclosed within this contemporary structure is the original Tyson-Derst Cottage which was built by Lawton Tyson from Savannah. It was then sold to the Derst family from Savannah who owned Derst Bakery.

47. THE HOPE HOUSE, c. 1920
121 Bridge Stree8

Built by the Causey family.

48. THE HANCOCK-LONG HOUSE, c. 1920
123 Bridge Street

This house was built in the early 1920s by Mary Baxter. She lived in the house until it was sold to Arthur Hancock in about 1928. In 1937 the "summer" kitchen was moved and attached to the main house. (See the Hope House in far right of photo.)

49. MERCER HOUSE, c.1937
127 Bridge Street

This house, built in 1937 by Mr. George Mercer of Savannah, Georgia, (the uncle of songwriter Johnny Mercer) was built as a brick "two over two" river cottage. A kitchen was attatched. Wooden portions were added by Mr. and Mrs. Ben Caldwell in the late 1970s.

Illustration by Naomi McCracken

On this property stood the cottages built in 1920s, where migrant workers lived who worked in the Lowden's Shell Mill. Still extant on the property is the only remaining Lowcountry barn, carefully restored by the recent owners.

50. OLD SHELL MILL, LOWDEN HOUSE & COTTAGE SITE
137 Bridge Street

All illustrations by Naomi McCracken

On this riverfront property next to Verdier Cove are the old Lowden House and Cottage.The Lowdens owned the mill on this site producing oysters, shrimp and crab meat. In addition the mill produced cracked oyster shells sold as fertilizer and chicken feed additive. A water tower for the plant is shown on the facing page.

This property was later owned by the Moses and the McCrackens and the Hancocks, and recently sold to the Dunaway and Vaux family.

Shell Mill, c. 1910

Water Tower, c. 1910

Return east on Bridge Street to Thomas Heyward Street and turn left.

51. NELLIE BROWN'S COTTAGE,
34 Heyward Street

Continue north on Heyward Street to May River Road and turn right.

52. HUGH O'QUINN COTTAGE,c. 1930
1256 May River Road

Mr. and Mrs. Hugh O'Quinn moved from Palmeton Bluff to Bluffton after the birth of their first child in 1928. He worked in the lumbering business through out the area. This is now the office of Kiser and Associates.

53. THE WILLIAMS COTTAGE, c. 1900
1251 May River Road

Built by Mrs. Lila Williams as a residence in 1900, this cottage has served for many years as the law offices of Vaux & Marscher.

54. THE DEER TONGUE WAREHOUSE, 1945 
1255 May River Road

Also known years ago as the Old Musk House, this commercial building was originally located across Huger Cove from the Seabrook House. It was built around 1945 by Eddie Mulligan and was placed behind his house on Calhoun Street. Built from used lumber and boards salvaged from an old factory in downtown Savannah, the structure is clad in crenellated metal.

Deer Tongue is a native plant that grew in the pine woods around Bluffton and in ditches throughout the Lowcountry. It was discovered by Dr. Joseph Mellichamp and used for medicinal purposes. Later, it was found that when air dried it emitted a pleasant fragrance which was used in perfumes, vanilla extract and later in tobacco. The building was relocated to May River Road in the 1980s and was renovated. In 1999, Roberts Vaux was awarded the BHPS Caldwell Award for it adaptive reuse.

55. THE BRUIN HOUSE, 1915
1281 May River Road

The builder of this pre WWI house is not clear from existing records. At one time the 9 acre tract was in the estate of Franklin E. Pope. Later owners included the Lawrence family and W. W. Simmons who sold seven and a half acres to Susan A. Perry of Savannah, who was probably a relative of B. L. Perry, the pastor of St. John's Baptist Church since his estate owned adjoining land. In April, 1935, she sold the parcel of land to Abraham Bruin.

56. THE FRANCIS COBURN LIQUOR STORE, C. 1940
May River Road

Known as the "Red Dot", this structure, with the appearance of a filling station, served as a liquor store until the 1980s. It was a wood frame structure built in the 1930s, and due to several robberies the building was bricked-up in the 1960s.

Continue on May River Road turn right at Boundary and return to the Heyward House.

BLUFFTON. S.C.

OUTLYING AREA HISTORIC STRUCTURES

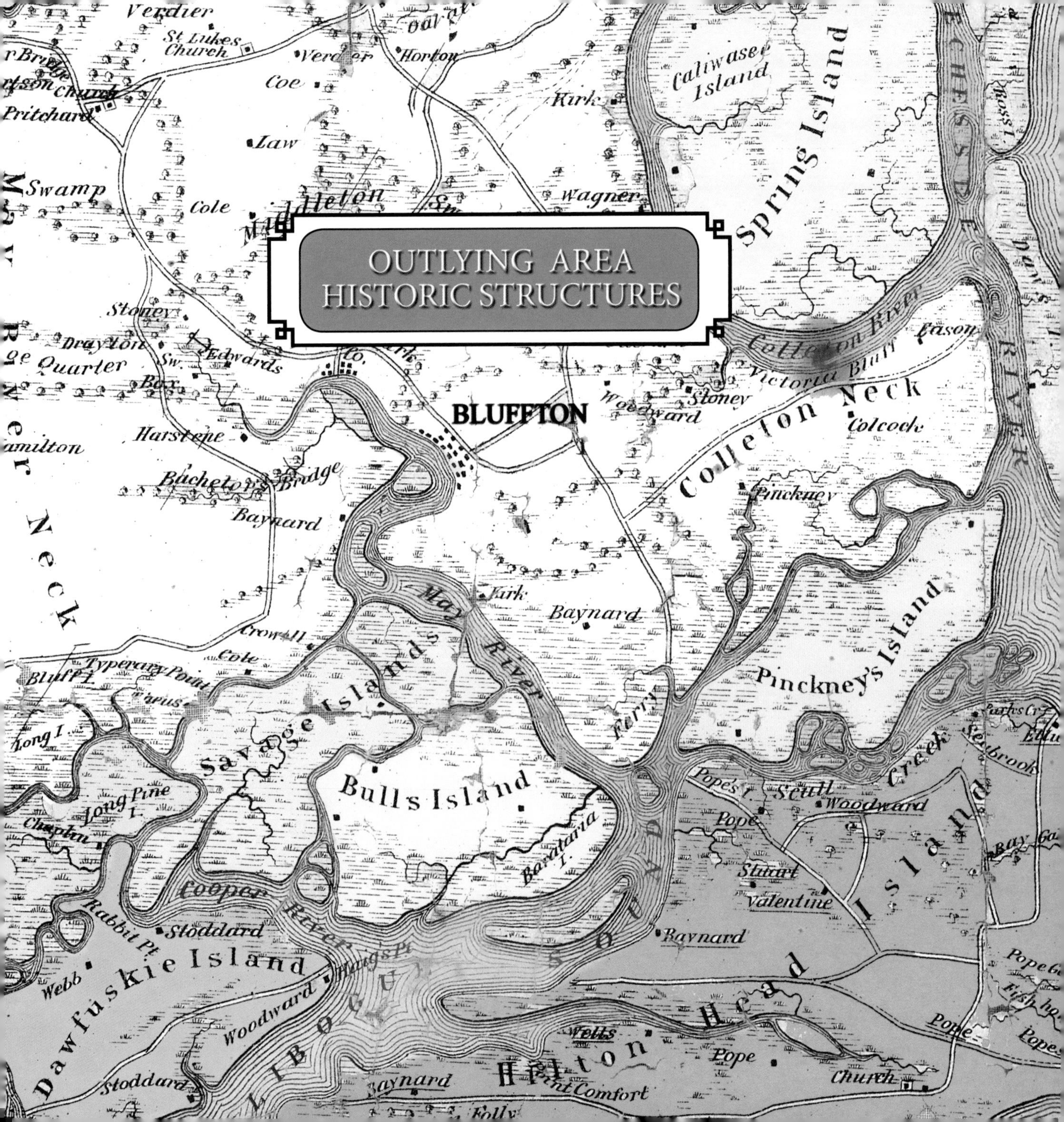

BLUFFTON

Verdier
St Lukes Church
Verdier
Horton
Coe
Pritchard
Law
Kirk
Caliwasee Island
Spring Island
Swamp
Cole
Middleton
Wagner
May River Neck
Stoney
Drayton
Quarter
Sw.
Edwards
Box
Colleton River
Victoria Bluff
Eason
Stoney
Woodward
Colleton Neck
Colcock
Harstene
Hamilton
Bachelor's Bridge
Baynard
Pinckney
Kirk
Baynard
May River
Crowell
Cole
Typerary Point
Bluff I.
Savage Islands
Pinckney's Island
Ferry
Long I.
Bulls Island
Pope's I.
Scull Creek
Seabrook
Woodward
Long Pine I.
Chaplin
Pope
Barataria I.
Stuart
Valentine
Cooper River
Rabbit Pt.
Stoddard
Baynard
Dawfuskie Island
Webb
Haigs Pt.
Woodward
Calibogue Sound
Hilton Head Island
Wells
Pope
Stoddard
Baynard
Point Comfort
Church
Pope
Folly

The Ike Brown Home

The Cahill Home

The Simmons Home

The Niver Home

To explore the outlying areas drive west on Highway 46 (towards Savannah) leaving the historic district of Bluffton

Palmetto Bluff

The Wilson Home on Palmetto Bluff was built in 1915 by Richard T Wilson, brother-in-law to Cornelius Vanderbuilt, Jr. With forty rooms it was rightfully regarded as the most palatial residence in the area. On March 2, 1926 it burned to the ground and only the columns remain.

The Johnson Home

Praise House

The Cannery

The Old Pritchardville Post Office

Turn right at the traffic circle at Highway 46 onto Highway 170

St. Luke's Church

In 1824 John Guerard, a wealthy planter, who lived in Saint Luke's Parish gave land for a new Episcopal church and it was completed in 1825. The church building was sold in 1875 for two hundred dollars to the Methodists and they have conducted services there since that date.

Barrel Landing School

On the river, just north of the gate to Highway 170, there once stood a small schoolhouse. The historic Barrel Landing School was built in the early 1800s and later became a community center and polling place.

Turn East toward Bluffton on Highway 278

Calhoun Plantation
Pinckney Colony Road

Rose Hill Mansion
Rose Hill Plantation, Highway 278

One of the eight original Lord Propriators of Carolina, Sir John Colleton, was granted the 12,000-acre Colleton Neck Barony in 1718. When the last Colleton died in 1828 James Kirk of Kirk's Bluff, now Bluffton, bought the property. His daughter, Caroline, and her husband Dr. John Kirk, built this Gothic Revival house in1859. They and their decendants lived there until 1928.

Continue down Highway 278 turn right onto Simmonsville Road

Praise House

Continue down Simmonsville Road to Highway 46

Brown Home

Go east from the Heyward House east on Bridge Street / Alljoy Road

Mayfair
Myrtle Island Road

The Lee Home
Myrtle Island Road

Historic Properties on Alljoy and Myrtle Island Roads

Lightsey Summer Cottage

The Old AllJoy Hotel (Burned 1945 and no longer exists)

BHPS BOOK SOURCES

Bluffton Historical Preservation Society Caldwell Archive, 48 Boundary Street, Bluffton, SC, collections of genealogy, history, photographs, books, documents and maps.

"The Longer Short History of Bluffton and Its Environs", Impression Printing Co. 1988.

"St. Luke's Parish Beaufort District South Carolina Census Records 1790 – 1900", Bluffton Historical Preservation Society, Inc. 1996.

" Historic Resources of the Low Country a Regional Survey of Beaufort County, SC, Colleton County, SC, Hampton County, SC, Jasper County, SC". Low Country Council of Governments, 2nd printing 1990.

National Register of Historic Places United States Department of the Interior, National Park Service Certification of Bluffton Historic District 1996.

Other Books

Burn, Billie, "An Island Names Daufuskie",The Reprint Company, 1991

Danielson, Michael N., " Profits and Politics in Paradise, The Development of Hilton Head Island". University of South Carolina Press, 1995.

Hefter, Natalie (editor), " Hilton Head Island, Images of America", Coastal Discovery Museum, 1998.

Marscher, Fran H.
" Remembering the Way It Was at Hilton Head, Bluffton and Daufuskie". The Historic Press, 2005.
" Remembering The Way It Was" volume two, The Historic Press, 2007
"Remembering the Way It Was at Beaufort, Sheldon and the Sea Islands", The Historic Press, 2006.

Powell, Mary P.
"Over Home", R.L Bryan Co., 1982
" Back Over Home", R. L. Bryan Co., 1996
" Back Home Roots", R. L. Bryan Co., 2005

Rowland, Lawrence S., Moore, Alexander and Rogers, George C.,Jr., "The History of Beaufort County, South Carolina, Volume 1,1514-1861".University of South Carolina Press, 1996

Maps

A Map of South Carolina and a Part of Georgia, William De Brahm, originally published by Jeffry's Co., London, England 1757. Bluffton Historical Preservation Society 2005 edition copyright.

South Carolina Plantations on the Savannah Back River 1851. Hand drawn map, Bluffton Historical Preservation Society copyright.

Strangers are exciting, their mystery never ends, but there's nothing like seeing your history in the faces of your friends.
- Ani DiFranco

House Numbers

1. The Cole-Heyward House
2. The Rate
3. The Guilford House
4. The Cantrell House
5. The Pine House
6. The Whitney Cottage
7. The Squire Pope Carriage House
8. Old Town Wharf Pavilion
9. The Church of the Cross
10. The Allen-Lockwood House
11. The Huger-Gordon House
12. Seven Oaks
13. The Graves House
14. The Fripp-Lowden House
15. The Store
16. The Mulligan House
17. The Dispensary Site
18. The Seabrook House
19. The Carson Cottage
20. The D. Hasell Heyward House
21. The Patz Brothers' House
22. The Planters Mercantile
23. The Cordray House
24. Old Bluffton Tabernacle
25. The Coastal Battery Housing
26. The Fripp House
27. The Card House
28. Heyward Cove Bridge
29. The Bluff
30. Prichard Street Park
31. The Prichard House
32. Old One Room School House
33. The Julia Joyner King Cottage
34. The Old Bruin Cottage
35. The Joyner House
36. Campbell Chapel AME Church
37. Board and Batten House
38. Caldwell Archives- BHPS
39. Beech House
40. Sarah Riley Hooks Cottage
41. Colcock-Teel House
42. Cedar Bluff
43. Orage Cottage
44. Bluffton Oyster Factory
45. The Hancock-Minor House
46. The Tyson-Derst Cottage
47. The Hope House
48. The Hancock-Long House
49. The Mercer House
50. Lowden House, Cottage & Old Shell Mill Site
51. Nellie Brown's Cottage
52. Hugh O'Quinn's Cottage
53. The Williams Cottage
54. The Deer Tongue Warehouse
55. The Bruin House
56. The Francis Coburn Liquor Store